God's Servant RUTH

A POEM WITH A PROMISE

DOUGLAS BOND

ILLUSTRATED BY MCKENNA SHAFFER

P&R PUBLISHING
P.O. BOX 817 • PHILLIPSBURG • NEW JERSEY 08865-0817

NAOMI LOSES EVERYTHING

Once in ancient Bible times,
In hot and arid desert climes,
There lived a clan from Bethlehem
Who had some sorrow fall on them;
But God had made a loving plan
To save them by his sovereign hand.

Now watch these folks from Israel
    On whom this sorrow fell,
As Yahweh, God their King,
    His lovingkindness brings.

Let's meet this clan from Israel,
    Where God's own children dwell:
Elimelech the patriarch,
    Naomi was the matriarch;
    Mahlon, he was their eldest son,
    And Chilion their youngest one.

The story that befell,
I am about to tell:
At first there was no rain,
And then there was no grain.
Without a grain of wheat,
They had no bread to eat
And nothing much to drink—
Their lives were on the brink!

It's famine! What disaster!
Soon blows fell fast and faster!

They heard that Moab had some bread.
"We need some bread!" Elimelech said.
They walked for days and days
Through barren desert, heat, and haze.

Until Elimelech got sick;
His head was sore, felt like a brick.
Naomi cared for him and tried
To heal him, but… he died.
Naomi, heartsick, mourned and cried.

Though her husband now was dead,
She stayed in Moab—they had bread.
Her sons both married foreign wives,
And all seemed better in their lives.

Until—
    Woe is me! There's more disaster,
    Following hard and following faster!

The Lord removed her firstborn son,
But he was not the only one;
Soon life was gone from Chilion.
Naomi's tears flowed on and on.

While grieving, empty, all alone,
Naomi only sighed and groaned.
Bereft of husband, sons, and clan,
Alone in pagan Moab's land,
    Naomi felt forsaken by God's hand.

Ruth Cleaves to Naomi

Then word arrived that Judah got some rain
And now had lots of wine and grain.
Naomi packed her things and made for home,
    But she was not alone.
Three widows traveled now, in truth;
    The youngest one was Ruth.

First Orpah said, "I'm coming too,"
And Ruth replied, "I'll stay with you."
Naomi told them it was kind
    But bid them stay behind.
"May God be good, as you have been,
    And bring you husbands from your kin."

The more Naomi tried,
The more her daughters wept and cried.
She gave them each a kiss,
And then she asked them this:
"If I had newborn sons right now,
Would you just sit and wait
To take your marriage vow
Until some far-off future date?

“If I had a husband tonight
And God gave me sons full of might,
I doubt you’d wait ’til they were grown!
Now, listen, daughters—go back home!”

The more Naomi tried,
The more her daughters wept and cried.

“It makes no sense—turn back!
Go home—turn back!
To your kin—turn back!
To your gods—turn back!”

Amidst the sniffles and the tears,
The eldest listened with her ears;
To Moab she turned back and left,
Of covenant kindness now bereft.

But Ruth refused to leave,
Resolved on Naomi to cleave.

"Your sister Orpah, she turned back;
In Moab she will nothing lack.
Dear Ruth, *dear Ruth!*—Turn back! Turn back!"

"Oh, urge me not; I'll never leave!
On you I will forever cleave!
I'll follow you—that's what I'll do:
Where you go, I will go;
Where you lodge, I will lodge;
Your clan, my clan;
Your God, my God;

"Naomi, hear my cry—
Where you die, I will die!

"May death alone tear us apart.
I swear it with my beating heart!
My name is Ruth—this is the truth!"

THE HOUSE OF BREAD

From pagan Moab Ruth was free;
That much was clear, Naomi could see.
To Israel's land they looked ahead,
To Bethlehem, the House of Bread.

Their steps they turned to the promised land,
Side by side and hand in hand;
For days they walked—long, weary days—
Through barren desert, heat, and haze.

When Bethlehem came into view,
The whole town formed a retinue.
"Who is this weary woman that we see?
Could it be—
Is it she—
Naomi with a visitor,
Both destitute and sore,
Pathetic, lonely, grieving, poor?"

"'Naomi' now is not my name;
I'm filled with bitterness and shame.
My life, once pleasant, full and free,
Is bitter now by God's decree.

"Full was I when I departed,
Hoping God would make me glad;
Now returned, I'm brokenhearted,
Battered, bitter, bruised, and sad,
Empty, lonely, feeling bad."

Naomi got a few things wrong,
But God turns bitterness to song.
Read on with me,
And you'll soon see:
Her God had made a loving plan
To save her by his sovereign hand.

It was her Father's kind behest
To bring her home for barley harvest.
He leads his children to their rest
And always gives them what is best.

Though widowed, hungry, short on hope,
Young Ruth didn't sit around and mope
Or pout and sulk and gripe.
The barley grain was ripe!

"It's harvest time; I can't complain—
I'll glean in the fields for grain!"

Kinsman-Redeemer

Ruth, whose life was spent with weepers,
Now found herself rejoicing with the reapers!
With reapers in a rich man's field,
Their kinsman would be soon revealed.

Now Boaz spoke to all his workers
And warned against them being shirkers:
"Make sure fair Ruth is treated well,
Her basket full with spare to sell."

He bowed his head to Ruth and said,
"Don't hesitate or stand in line;
Come, dip a morsel in the wine."

Determined not to leave her to her fate,
With roasted grain he heaped Ruth's plate.
Her life had been so sorrowful,
Yet here she was so dutiful,
So loyal and so beautiful—
Good Boaz thought that Ruth was wonderful!

To his reapers he entreated,
And oftentimes repeated,
"Let Ruth alone to glean;
Be sure her sack is full and never lean;
Be sure not one of you is ever mean."

While gleaning barley, threshing wheat,
Naomi and Ruth had plenty to eat.

And then a strange event occurred—
Stranger than you've ever heard:
While resting on the threshing floor,
Boaz had a visitor.

By ancient custom, love was sworn
Right there amidst the barleycorn.
Their holy tryst was pure and chaste,
But Boaz had no time to waste.

Now Boaz was a little stressed;
He knew there was one further test.
There was a closer relative,
Who had the first prerogative.
He formed a plan and sat down at the gate
Where all the elders congregate.

"Redeemer, friends, draw near;
Please take a seat right here.

"Naomi the widow is selling her land."
He paused. "The land is owned by her clan.
And with the land belongs the hand
(I would not lie—this is the truth)
Of Lot's granddaughter Ruth.

"For Ruth the foreign Moabite,
Will you, her kinsman, do what's right?
No doubt she is your trueborn kin,
Though she has pagan blood mixed in.

"The duty of the man, forsooth,
Of the one who marries Ruth,
Is having sons who will reclaim
And carry on the family name:
'Elimelech,' who's been denied
His land and name because he died.
Such is the case, in truth,
For he who marries Ruth."

While frowning and stroking his beard,
The kinsman-redeemer feared:
"Imperil my inheritance?
Not likely in such circumstance,
Without a glance—and no romance—
No, I won't do it—not a chance!"

Relieved, good Boaz wiped his head,
And cleared his throat, and said,
"Then I will buy Naomi's land,
And with the land, the widow's hand—
I swear it by my life!
Oh, dear Ruth—would you, could you, be my wife?"

Now Ruth thought he was wonderful!
Naomi thought him bountiful!
Their God had made a better plan
To rescue their entire clan!

Then nine months later God gave Ruth
(This really happened—it's the truth)
A strapping, bouncing baby boy!
Oh, how his parents sang for joy!

"All praise and blessing, adoration,
Redeemer Lord of our salvation!"

(Do you wonder what they named the tyke?
Not Phil, or Bill, or Mike,
Not Boaz, Bob, or Fred.
Instead they smiled and said,
"Let's call him baby Obed!")

Now far behind Ruth was disaster.
For grace flowed fast and faster,
Unmeasured mercy from her Master!

A thousand years long after them,
Naomi's clan in Bethlehem,
On the first and merriest Advent morn,
The Christ, Redeemer King, was born!

THE GOSPEL TRUTH ABOUT RUTH

Since Ruth came from a pagan Moabite
And Boaz from a harlot Canaanite,
To all the nations, tribes, and tongues
Unmeasured lovingkindness runs.

The God of sovereign grace and might
    Has pitched his love on Israelites
    And chosen pagan Girgashites,
    The Hittite and the Perizzite,
    The Jebusite and Moabite—
In all the nations God delights!

O blessed be the God of Israel!
Who kindness pours on infidels,
Redeems our souls from death and hell,
And makes us heirs, with Christ to dwell.

While fully God and fully man,
From shameful parentage and pagan clan,
Ordained by God's mysterious plan,
Came forth the blessed Son of Man!

So, children, God wants you to know—
        To rescue you from sin and woe—
How wide-embracing love and mercy go.
Mysterious purposes they be
That God redeems both you and me!

All praise and glory, adoration,
O Sovereign Lord, from all creation!

Remember, children, let's agree,
That God in heaven by decree,
        Established his redeeming plan
        To save his children by his hand.

Now, just before we sing,
Agree on one more thing:
        What troubles do for folks like Ruth
        Is pour out Jesus' gospel truth!

Not Jew nor Gentile

We worship Christ, the Cornerstone,
Who made us one in him alone!
Not Jew nor Gentile, bond nor free,
This commonwealth of unity.
Our Lord has from the two made one,
And with his blood our peace has won.

Brought near in Christ, the Prince of Peace,
Our envy, strife, and warfare cease;
For tribes and tongues, and strangers all,
Our Peace has broken down the wall;
Redeeming mercy he extends
To us his fellow heirs and friends.

One faith, one hope of heav'n above,
A unity of holy love;
One body made of many parts,
A unity of loving hearts;
One temple built of cast-off stone,
Made holy by the Holy One.

To Jesus Christ we lift one voice—
The household of our Father's choice—
Whose love makes ours for others grow
And makes the watching world to know
That our redeeming Cornerstone
Has made us one in Christ alone!

Ask your parents to go to bondbooks.net/hymns
so you can sing along.

Big Words (Like "Kin")

Arid: The climate of a dry place with little or no rain.
Behest: A person's order or command.
Bereft: The loss of something good.
Brink: The moment when something bad is about to happen.
Clan: A community of close-knit families.
Cleave: To stick with someone with unwavering loyalty.
Decree(s): "The decrees of God are his eternal purpose, according to the counsel of his will, whereby, for his own glory, he hath foreordained whatsoever comes to pass." (Westminster Shorter Catechism, answer 7)
Disaster: A sudden event that causes great damage or loss of life.
Forsooth: In truth; indeed.
Glean: The act of gathering the leftovers of a crop after the farmer has finished harvesting.
Harlot: A woman who lives with men as if she were married to them even though none of them are her husband.
Heir: The person who has the right to the wealth of another.
Infidel: A person who does not believe in the one true God.
Kin: A relative.
Lest: Preventing or avoiding the risk of something undesirable.
Matriarch: The mother.
Pagan: Someone who believes in false gods.
Patriarch: The father.
Prerogative: A right or privilege.
Retinue: A group of people.
Romance: When your mommy and daddy hold hands, hug, and kiss.
Sheaves: A bundle of grain stalks tied together after reaping.
Shirker: Someone who tries to get out of doing work (like cleaning your room or washing the dishes).
Sovereign: A name that refers to God as the King of Kings.

Tryst: A romantic meeting between a man and a woman.
Tyke: A Middle English word meaning "small child."
Yahweh: The one true God of Israel, revealed to Moses as four Hebrew consonants: YHWH.

Let's Think!

1. What town was Naomi originally from?
2. What else would happen many years later in that same town?
3. Why did Naomi and her family leave Israel?
4. What were some of the bad things that happened to her family? Have any bad things happened in your family?
5. In what ways did God show his faithfulness to Naomi and Ruth?
6. They returned to Israel during the ______________ harvest.
7. In whose field did Ruth glean?
8. Moms and dads, look up Matthew 1:1–17, especially verse 5. Discuss how God's perfect plan of redemption includes the minutest details of parentage and genealogy.
9. Read Romans 8:28 out loud. How should we respond when bad things happen?
10. What were ways God used unlikely people to bring about his saving plan?
11. What is the sovereign plan that God reveals in the book of Ruth?

For my children and grandchildren—
and all who long for the Kinsman-Redeemer.

ISBN: 978-1-59638-760-7 (hbk)
ISBN: 978-1-59638-761-4 (ePub)

Printed in the United States of America

Library of Congress Cataloging-in-Publication Data

Names: Bond, Douglas, 1958- author. | Shaffer, McKenna, illustrator.
Title: God's servant Ruth : a poem with a promise / Douglas Bond ; illustrated by McKenna Shaffer.
Description: Phillipsburg : P&R Publishing, 2023. | Audience: Ages 5-12 | Audience: Grades 4-6 | Summary: "God's Servant Ruth tells the story of Naomi, Boaz, and Ruth in verse. This beautifully illustrated book explains foundational theology for younger children as it points to a glorious Redeemer"-- Provided by publisher.
Identifiers: LCCN 2023000789 | ISBN 9781596387607 (hardback) | ISBN 9781596387614 (epub)
Subjects: LCSH: Ruth (Biblical figure)--Juvenile literature. | Naomi (Biblical figure)--Juvenile literature. | Boaz (Biblical figure)--Juvenile literature.
Classification: LCC BS580.R8 B66 2023 | DDC 222/.35--dc23/eng/20230519
LC record available at https://lccn.loc.gov/2023000789